REFLECTIONS
FOR
LENT 2022

REFLECTIONS
FOR
LENT

2 March – 16 April 2022

CHRISTOPHER HERBERT
PHILIP NORTH
ANGELA TILBY
RACHEL TREWEEK

with Holy Week reflections by
ROWAN WILLIAMS

and an introduction by
MARK OAKLEY

Church House Publishing
Church House
Great Smith Street
London SW1P 3AZ

ISBN 978 1 78140 276 4

Published 2021 by Church House Publishing
Copyright © The Archbishops' Council 2021

The opinions expressed in this book are those of the
authors and do not necessarily reflect the official policy of
the General Synod or The Archbishops' Council of the
Church of England.

Liturgical editor: Peter Moger
Series editor: Hugh Hillyard-Parker
Designed and typeset by Hugh Hillyard-Parker
Copyedited by Ros Connelly
Printed and bound by
CPI Group (UK) Ltd, Croydon, CR0 4YY

What do you think of *Reflections for Lent*?

We'd love to hear from you – simply email us at

publishing@churchofengland.org

or write to us at

Church House Publishing, Church House,
Great Smith Street, London SW1P 3AZ.

Visit **www.dailyprayer.org.uk** for more
information on the *Reflections* series, ordering
and subscriptions.

Contents

About the authors

Stephen Cottrell is the Archbishop of York, having previously been Bishop of Chelmsford. He is a well-known writer and speaker on evangelism, spirituality and catechesis. He is one of the team that produced *Pilgrim*, the popular course for the Christian Journey.

Christopher Herbert was ordained in Hereford in 1967, becoming a curate and then Diocesan Director of Education. He was an incumbent in Surrey and later, Archdeacon of Dorking. Appointed Bishop of St Albans, he retired in 2009.

Philip North is the Bishop of Burnley. He has spent much of his ministry in urban and estates parishes in the Dioceses of Durham and London, and has also served as Priest Administrator of the Shrine of Our Lady of Walsingham. He is a member of the Company of Mission Priests.

Mark Oakley is Dean and Fellow of St John's College, Cambridge, and Honorary Canon Theologian of Wakefield Cathedral in the Diocese of Leeds. He is the author of *The Collage of God* (2001), *The Splash of Words: Believing in Poetry* (2016), and *My Sour Sweet Days: George Herbert and the Journey of the Soul* (2019) as well as articles and reviews, in the areas of faith, poetry, human rights and literature. He is Visiting Lecturer in the department of Theology and Religious Studies at King's College London.

Angela Tilby is a Canon Emeritus of Christ Church Cathedral, Oxford, and Canon of Honour at Portsmouth Cathedral. Prior to that she served in the Diocese of Oxford following a period in Cambridge, where she was at Westcott House and St Bene't's Church. Before ordination she was a producer for the BBC, and she still broadcasts regularly.

Rachel Treweek is Bishop of Gloucester and the first female diocesan bishop in England. She served in two parishes in London and was Archdeacon of Northolt and later Hackney. Prior to ordination she was a speech and language therapist and is a trained practitioner in conflict transformation.

Rowan Williams was born and brought up in Wales, and worked in pastoral and academic settings in Cambridge and Oxford before becoming Bishop of Monmouth in 1992. He was Archbishop of Canterbury from 2002 to 2012, and is the author of over 30 books on theology, spirituality, literature and current issues.

About *Reflections for Lent*

Based on the *Common Worship Lectionary* readings for Morning Prayer, these daily reflections are designed to refresh and inspire times of personal prayer. The aim is to provide rich, contemporary and engaging insights into Scripture.

Each page lists the lectionary readings for the day, with the main psalms for that day highlighted in **bold**. The collect of the day – either the *Common Worship* collect or the shorter additional collect – is also included.

For those using this book in conjunction with a service of Morning Prayer, the following conventions apply: a psalm printed in parentheses is omitted if it has been used as the opening canticle at that office; a psalm marked with an asterisk may be shortened if desired.

A short reflection is provided on either the Old or New Testament reading. Popular writers, experienced ministers, biblical scholars and theologians contribute to this series, all bringing their own emphases, enthusiasms and approaches to biblical interpretation.

Regular users of Morning Prayer and *Time to Pray* (from *Common Worship: Daily Prayer*) and anyone who follows the Lectionary for their regular Bible reading will benefit from the rich variety of traditions represented in these stimulating and accessible pieces.

The book also includes both a simple form of Common Worship: Morning Prayer (see pages 48–49) and a short form of Night Prayer, also known as Compline (see pages 52–55), particularly for the benefit of those readers who are new to the habit of the Daily Office or for any reader while travelling.

Lent – jousting within the self

It has been said that the heart of the human problem is the problem of the human heart. Lent is time set aside each year to take this thought seriously.

A few years ago, there was a story in the papers about a painting by Pieter Bruegel the Elder. It is currently on display in Vienna's marvellous Kunsthistorisches Museum, but Krakow's National Museum claims it is theirs and that it was stolen by the wife of the city's Nazi governor in 1939 during the occupation of Poland.

The painting is called 'The Fight Between Carnival and Lent' and it was painted in 1559. It is a beautifully typical Bruegel painting. It is a large, crowded canvas with nearly 200 men, women and children depicted on it. We find ourselves looking down on a town square during a riotous festival. The painting can be looked at in two halves. On the right, we see a church with people leaving after prayer. We see them giving alms to the poor, feeding the hungry, helping those with disability, calling attention to their need and tending to the dying. On the left, we see an inn. Congregated around it are beer drinkers, gamblers, various saucy types. The vulnerable nearby are not noticed, including a solitary procession of lepers. Instead, a man vomits out of a window and another bangs his head against a wall.

In the foreground, we see two figures being pulled towards each other on floats. One is Lady Lent, gaunt and unshowy, dressed as a nun, with followers eating pretzels and fish as well as drawing fresh water from a large well. The other is Carnival, a fat figure, armed with a meat spit and a pork pie helmet. He's followed by masked carousers. A man in yellow – the symbolic colour of deceit – pushes his float, though he looks rather weighed down by cups and a bag of belongings. In the background, we see, on the left, some stark, leafless trees, but on the right side, buds are awakening on the branches and, as if to see them better, a woman is busily cleaning her windows.

It is an allegorical delight, and we might do worse than take a close look at it sometime this Lent. It's tempting to classify each human there as either good or bad, secular or faithful, kind or indifferent. We love to place people into convenient cutlery trays, dividing us all up as is most useful for us. What I love about this painting, however, is that it reminds me that we are all similarly made with two halves.

For so many of us, there is a constant fight going on within between the times we are negligent and the times we are careful; days in which we get through with a self that enjoys its own attention, being centre-stage, and days when our self just feels somehow more itself when not being selfish. I have an impulse to pray; I have an impulse to avoid or forget it. There are parts of me grotesquely masked, and there are parts of me trying to clean my windows on a ladder, as it were, wanting to increase transparency and attention to the world, to me and to my relationships.

Lent begins with a small dusty cross being made on my head, the hard case that protects the organ that makes decisions. The season starts by asking me to imagine how life might be if the imprint of Christ's courageous compassion might make itself felt and acted on, rather than just passionately talked about. Lent knows what we are like. It has seen the painting. It has read a bit of Freud, some history books, political manifestos and memoirs of hurt and achievement. It winces at our cyclical, self-destructive repetitions. It believes in us, though, knowing that, with God and each other, if we reach outside of our own hardened little worlds, we set the scene to be helped and, maybe, even changed. That would be good – for me and those who live with me.

In the Gospels, the 40 days Jesus spent in the beguiling wilderness immediately followed his baptism. Coming up out of the water, he had heard the unmistakable voice that matters, telling him he was cherished, wanted and ready. He then goes into the heat spending time with himself, hearing other voices that want him to live down to them; but he knows that his vocation can only be lived when he learns to live up to the one voice he heard that day in the river, not down to the ones that want him to live some conventionally indifferent and submerged existence as a consumer of the world and not as a citizen of the kingdom. We follow him. Where he goes, so do we. A wilderness Lent is needed more than ever to do some heart-repair and start becoming Christians again.

I don't know who owns the Bruegel painting. What I do know is that its themes belong to all of us; our inner landscape matches his rowdy town square. As long as the fight continues, the soul will be alive.

Mark Oakley

3

Building daily prayer into daily life

In our morning routines there are many tasks we do without giving much thought to them, and others that we do with careful attention. Daily prayer and Bible reading is a strange mixture of these. These are disciplines (and gifts) that we as Christians should have in our daily pattern, but they are not tasks to be ticked off. Rather they are a key component of our developing relationship with God. In them is *life* – for the fruits of this time are to be lived out by us – and to be most fruitful, the task requires both purpose and letting go.

In saying a daily office of prayer, we make a deliberate decision to spend time with God – the God who is always with us. In prayer and attentive reading of the Scriptures, there is both a conscious entering into God's presence and a 'letting go' of all we strive to control: both are our acknowledgement that it is God who is God.

> *… come before his presence with a song…*
>
> *Know that the Lord is God;*
> *it is he that has made us and we are his;*
> *we are his people and the sheep of his pasture.*
>
> *Enter his gates with thanksgiving…*
>
> *(Psalm 100, a traditional Canticle at Morning Prayer)*

If we want a relationship with someone to deepen and grow, we need to spend time with that person. It can be no surprise that the same is true between us and God.

In our daily routines, I suspect that most of us intentionally look in the mirror; occasionally we might see beyond the surface of our external reflection and catch a glimpse of who we truly are. For me, a regular pattern of daily prayer and Bible reading is like a hard look in a clean mirror: it gives a clear reflection of myself, my life and the world in which I live. But it is more than that, for in it I can also see the reflection of God who is most clearly revealed in Jesus Christ and present with us now in the Holy Spirit.

This commitment to daily prayer is about our relationship with the God who is love. St Paul, in his great passage about love, speaks of now seeing 'in a mirror, dimly' but one day seeing face to face: 'Now I know only in part; then I will know fully, even as I have been fully known' (1 Corinthians 13.12). Our daily prayer is part of that seeing in a mirror dimly, and it is also part of our deep yearning for an ever-clearer vision of our God. As we read Scripture, the past and the future converge in the present moment. We hear words from long ago – some of which can appear strange and confusing – and yet, the Holy Spirit is living and active in the present. In this place of relationship and revelation, we open ourselves to the possibility of being changed, of being reshaped in a way that is good for us and all creation.

It is important that the words of prayer and scripture should penetrate deep within rather than be a mere veneer. A quiet location is therefore a helpful starting point. For some, domestic circumstances or daily schedule make that difficult, but it is never impossible to become more fully present to God. The depths of our being can still be accessed no matter the world's clamour and activity. An awareness of this is all part of our journey from a false sense of control to a place of letting go, to a place where there is an opportunity for transformation.

Sometimes in our attention to Scripture there will be connection with places of joy or pain; we might be encouraged or provoked or both. As we look and see and encounter God more deeply, there will be thanksgiving and repentance; the cries of our heart will surface as we acknowledge our needs and desires for ourselves and the world. The liturgy of Morning Prayer gives this voice and space.

I find it helpful to begin Morning Prayer by lighting a candle. This marks my sense of purpose and my acknowledgement of Christ's presence with me. It is also a silent prayer for illumination as I prepare to be attentive to what I see in the mirror, both of myself and of God. Amid the revelation of Scripture and the cries of my heart, the constancy of the tiny flame bears witness to the hope and light of Christ in all that is and will be.

When the candle is extinguished, I try to be still as I watch the smoke disappear. For me, it is symbolic of my prayers merging with the day. I know that my prayer and the reading of Scripture are not the smoke and mirrors of delusion. Rather, they are about encounter and discovery as I seek to venture into the day to love and serve the Lord as a disciple of Jesus Christ.

+ Rachel Treweek

Lectio Divina – a way of reading the Bible

Lectio Divina is a contemplative way of reading the Bible. It dates back to the early centuries of the Christian Church and was established as a monastic practice by Benedict in the sixth century. It is a way of praying the Scriptures that leads us deeper into God's word. We slow down. We read a short passage more than once. We chew it over slowly and carefully. We savour it. Scripture begins to speak to us in a new way. It speaks to us personally, and aids that union we have with God through Christ, who is himself the Living Word.

Make sure you are sitting comfortably. Breathe slowly and deeply. Ask God to speak to you through the passage that you are about to read.

This way of praying starts with our silence. We often make the mistake of thinking prayer is about what we say to God. It is actually the other way round. God wants to speak to us. He will do this through the Scriptures. So don't worry about what to say. Don't worry if nothing jumps out at you at first. God is patient. He will wait for the opportunity to get in. He will give you a word and lead you to understand its meaning for you today.

First reading: Listen
As you read the passage listen for a word or phrase that attracts you. Allow it to arise from the passage as if it is God's word for you today. Sit in silence repeating the word or phrase in your head.

Then say the word or phrase aloud.

Second reading: Ponder
As you read the passage again, ask how this word or phrase speaks to your life and why it has connected with you. Ponder it carefully. Don't worry if you get distracted – it may be part of your response to offer to God. Sit in silence and then frame a single sentence that begins to say aloud what this word or phrase says to you.

Third reading: Pray

As you read the passage for the last time, ask what Christ is calling from you. What is it that you need to do or consider or relinquish or take on as a result of what God is saying to you in this word or phrase? In the silence that follows the reading, pray for the grace of the Spirit to plant this word in your heart.

If you are in a group, talk for a few minutes and pray with each other.

If you are on your own, speak your prayer to God either aloud or in the silence of your heart.

If there is time, you may even want to read the passage a fourth time, and then end with the same silence before God with which you began.

++Stephen Cottrell

Wednesday 2 March
Ash Wednesday

Psalm **38**
Daniel 9.3-6, 17-19
1 Timothy 6.6-19

Daniel 9.3-6, 17-19

'... sinned and done wrong, acted wickedly and rebelled' (v.5)

We live in a culture that values unconditional positivity. We are expected to affirm, to encourage and to build up the self-esteem of those around us. And yet today, in churches across the world, priests will sign their people with ash using words that do the precise opposite. 'Remember you are dust, and to dust you will return.'

It is a brutal reminder of the hard truth that most people spend their lives running away from. Without God, we are nothing. Mere accidents of evolution, taunted by consciousness, living short and brutish lives, destined for annihilation. Yet the moment we accept our dependence upon him, God forgives us and changes us.

In chapter 9, Daniel accepts his own dependence on the Lord and turns to him in the deepest possible contrition. As he ponders the ruins of exilic Jerusalem, he speaks on behalf of a repentant nation, punished for their sin, for he knows that restoration can only come though the action of God.

In Lent, Daniel's contrite prayer becomes our own. It is the season to name and deal with sin, to confess our own apartness from God, our wilful rebellion and greed, our arrogant pride. For it is only through the gracious action of God who sent his Son to die for us that our lives make any sense. Without him, we are as much dust as the ruins of Jerusalem. Yet through our contrition, our lives are remade. For those who acknowledge their need, the New Jerusalem awaits.

COLLECT

Almighty and everlasting God,
you hate nothing that you have made
and forgive the sins of all those who are penitent:
create and make in us new and contrite hearts
that we, worthily lamenting our sins
and acknowledging our wretchedness,
may receive from you, the God of all mercy,
perfect remission and forgiveness;
through Jesus Christ your Son our Lord,
who is alive and reigns with you,
in the unity of the Holy Spirit,
one God, now and for ever.

Reflection by **Philip North**

Psalm **77** *or* 90, **92**
Genesis 39
Galatians 2.11-end

Thursday 3 March

Genesis 39

'Joseph's master took him and put him into the prison' (v.20)

Truth is costly. It entails sacrifice and pain and so can always be found walking hand in hand with suffering. That is what Joseph learns in his dealings with the Potiphar family.

It would have been so much easier if Joseph had just slept with Potiphar's wife. A well-concealed and doubtless juicy affair would have increased his popularity and given him power over the whole household. But Joseph chooses the path of truth and as a result finds himself in gaol.

What is striking in this narrative is that Joseph, who later wears his emotions very much on his sleeve, is so lacking in self-pity. He seems to accept the trials and tribulations of life with the carefree insouciance of a character in an Evelyn Waugh novel. That's because he trusts deeply in God and so knows that if he speaks and lives the truth, he will be vindicated. That vindication may take time, but it will come.

Dishonesty is a highly attractive temptation for all of us because it provides quick fix solutions to difficult problems. That is why so many people drift into deceitful behaviour without even properly thinking it through.

By contrast, truth is a long-term strategy that will often entail short-term pain and sacrifice. But God is truth, and he will always vindicate the one who bears the cost of truth. That vindication may be slow. But it will come.

Holy God,
our lives are laid open before you:
rescue us from the chaos of sin
and through the death of your Son
bring us healing and make us whole
in Jesus Christ our Lord.

COLLECT

Reflection by **Philip North**   9

Friday 4 March

Genesis 40

'Do not interpretations belong to God?' (v.8)

How can we tell what the future holds? In ancient Egypt, a chief method was through the interpretation of dreams. The butler and the baker, both imprisoned by Pharaoh, would have been desperate to know their future as revealed to them by their vivid dreams of grapes and baskets, but they were denied access to the skilled magicians and wise men who could have performed the task.

They would not have expected to find a solution in a fellow prisoner, let alone a Hebrew, but Joseph cheekily comes to their rescue. He may not have any training, but, he asks, 'Do not interpretations belong to God?'

Behind that simple question there lies the most massive theological claim. If God can interpret dreams, then the future must lie in God's hands. Joseph is claiming the sovereignty of the God of the Hebrews over all time and eternity.

Today, as Christians, we have no need for diviners or dream interpreters to tell the future. That future is revealed to us by the dying and rising of Jesus; it is set forth in the Scriptures and in the creeds and teachings of the Church. The future is Christ and the fullness of life in him. It is he who meets us in the prison cell of our mortality and sets us free. We can know for sure that all in the end will be glory.

COLLECT

Almighty and everlasting God,
you hate nothing that you have made
and forgive the sins of all those who are penitent:
create and make in us new and contrite hearts
that we, worthily lamenting our sins
and acknowledging our wretchedness,
may receive from you, the God of all mercy,
perfect remission and forgiveness;
through Jesus Christ your Son our Lord,
who is alive and reigns with you,
in the unity of the Holy Spirit,
one God, now and for ever.

Reflection by **Philip North**

Psalm 71 *or* 96, **97**, 100
Genesis 41.1-24
Galatians 3.15-22

Saturday 5 March

Genesis 41.1-24

'It is not I; God will give Pharaoh a favourable answer.' (v.16)

Joseph is taken before Pharaoh, and in just a few moments, the most formidable structures of power are utterly subverted.

This is a remarkable scene. For years Joseph has been languishing away in a filthy prison cell, forgotten by everyone but never losing his trust in God. Then all of a sudden, he shaves, gets a haircut, changes his clothes and finds himself before Pharaoh who shares with him the deepest secrets of his heart. Only Joseph can interpret the traumatic dream. The most powerful man on the planet needs the jailbird.

How can this be? Because Joseph speaks in the name of the God whose power utterly subverts all the structures and institutions conceived through the human mind. As St Paul would later write: 'Has not God made foolish the wisdom of the world?' (1 Corinthians 1.20)

We live in a world in which the colossal global strongholds of political power, military might and corporate dominance seem all pervasive – a world in which the gentle teaching of a roving preacher who lived 2,000 years ago in Galilee can so swiftly be drowned out or perceived as irrelevant.

But just as mighty Pharaoh needed the jailbird, so even the powers of the twenty-first century need with all their hearts the man nailed to the cross. For his wisdom makes foolish the wisdom of the world, and in him alone is life.

Holy God,
our lives are laid open before you:
rescue us from the chaos of sin
and through the death of your Son
bring us healing and make us whole
in Jesus Christ our Lord.

COLLECT

Reflection by **Philip North** | 11

Monday 7 March

Psalms 10, 11 *or* 98, 99, 101
Genesis 41.25-45
Galatians 3.23 – 4.7

Genesis 41.25-45

'See, I have set you over all the land of Egypt' (v.41)

The passage ends with Joseph elevated to a position of power with seemingly every human need provided for. Many would see that as a dream come true, yet the passage began with a very different sort of dream.

In the interpretation of Pharaoh's strange dream, Joseph has God-given insight into some important aspects of the future and is able to offer wisdom about preparing well for the years ahead. Yet this is far from altruistic. There is a strong sense of Pharaoh's desire to understand in order to be in control of the future, and Joseph is to be a partner in that. That theme of control has never been far from the surface throughout the Genesis narrative of Jacob and sons.

Lent is a time of preparation and there is a challenge for us in how we look beyond the immediate surface of the present to seek God's wisdom about how to live it well for the good of the future. However, despite endless forecasting and interpretation of data, we cannot predict or control all that lies ahead, but we can prayerfully pay attention to how what we do and are in the present will contribute to the shaping of the future and a vision of wellbeing for all people.

Our actions, choices and decisions today will have implications for tomorrow and beyond.

COLLECT

Almighty God,
whose Son Jesus Christ fasted forty days in the wilderness,
and was tempted as we are, yet without sin:
give us grace to discipline ourselves in obedience to your Spirit;
and, as you know our weakness,
so may we know your power to save;
through Jesus Christ your Son our Lord,
who is alive and reigns with you,
in the unity of the Holy Spirit,
one God, now and for ever.

Reflection by **Rachel Treweek**

Psalm **44** *or* **106*** (*or* 103)   **Tuesday 8 March**
Genesis 41.46 – 42.5
Galatians 4.8-20

Genesis 41.46 – 42.5

'The second he named Ephraim, "For God has made me fruitful in the land of my misfortunes."' (41.52)

This next episode brings into sharp relief the truth that there are many different layers of narrative at any particular point in time. This passage tells something of the big story of what is going on in the world regarding famine and Egypt's response; then against this panoramic backdrop, there is the detail of individual lives set within relationship in different locations. Names are both prominent and important, and all of it has something to say about identity. Interestingly, the names of Joseph's children reflect the threads of his own story. His seeming happiness in the present cannot be separated from the pain of the past. The story is not over yet.

In all of this we are reminded of the connectedness of our own story regarding people, place and time. There is mess and brokenness as well as beauty and yet somehow it is mysteriously held in the overarching story of God's purposes.

We each have a name and a unique identity with a story, past and present, lived out in specific places, and yet we are part of a bigger story that spans not only the world but time itself. God's creative work continues in our present within both the loveliness and the ugliness, rooted in what God has done through Christ in the past and the promise of what is to come. The story is not yet finished.

Heavenly Father,
your Son battled with the powers of darkness,
and grew closer to you in the desert:
help us to use these days to grow in wisdom and prayer
that we may witness to your saving love
in Jesus Christ our Lord.

COLLECT

Reflection by **Rachel Treweek**   13

Wednesday 9 March

Genesis 42.6-17

'Joseph also remembered...' (v.9)

As we engage with the next scene in the dramatic saga, we have narrative and speech, but it is devoid of any reference to emotions. Yet behind all these words there is much going on within people's hearts. The one tiny hint of this is in those words 'Joseph also remembered ...' Many years previously, Joseph's dreams had revealed a time when his brothers would bow down to him; his interpretation had ignited strong anger and jealousy within his siblings, provoking them to ruthless action to dispose of him.

Now, as Joseph recognizes his brothers, his response to the human visceral reaction is not one of fond reunion but rather something more akin to spiteful revenge. Once he had suffered at their exercise of power and control, and now it is their turn. There is irony in the use of the word 'remembering' because what Joseph recalls is a *dis*membering and an intentional tearing of familial bonds.

While there is the potential for a true re-membering, Joseph is perhaps understandably not yet in a place to live reconciliation, but these are dangerous moments as Joseph chooses to opt for manipulation and a power game.

How might you more deeply recognize the powerful emotions within you sparked by particular events or actions and pay careful attention to the choices you make in the light of them? Can you choose a re-membering rather than something potentially dangerous and destructive?

COLLECT

Almighty God,
whose Son Jesus Christ fasted forty days in the wilderness,
and was tempted as we are, yet without sin:
give us grace to discipline ourselves in obedience to your Spirit;
and, as you know our weakness,
so may we know your power to save;
through Jesus Christ your Son our Lord,
who is alive and reigns with you,
in the unity of the Holy Spirit,
one God, now and for ever.

14 | *Reflection by* **Rachel Treweek**

Psalms **42**, 43 *or* 113, **115**
Genesis 42.18-28
Galatians 5.2-15

Thursday 10 March

Genesis 42.18-28
'That is why this anguish has come upon us' (v.21)

Seeing trauma and turbulence as divine punishment is never a life-giving place to begin; it often leads to blame and finger-pointing rather than opening up the question about how we might live the present well in the light of the past and looking forwards. This is an important question for us and not one we yet see being asked by Joseph and his brothers.

The past is dominating the present and Joseph is determined to continue his game of one-upmanship; at the same time, the brothers are not yet willing to openly name their abhorrent dark secret.

However, we do begin to see human vulnerability cracking open new possibilities. For the first time, Joseph hears something of his brothers' regret and anguish as they acknowledge hearing his. Until now, they have all failed to hear the cries of each other's hearts and look at things through each other's eyes.

Perhaps Joseph's weeping is not only because the remembering is surfacing but also because he now sees the human brokenness in his brothers and can reframe what he once saw as only hard-hearted cruelty.

We are not asked to ignore people's abhorrent past actions, but it is important that we don't fail to see our own brokenness too. Repentance frees us to love not only love ourselves more deeply but also our neighbour. It is all rooted in first allowing God to love us.

Heavenly Father,
your Son battled with the powers of darkness,
and grew closer to you in the desert:
help us to use these days to grow in wisdom and prayer
that we may witness to your saving love
in Jesus Christ our Lord.

COLLECT

Reflection by **Rachel Treweek**

Friday 11 March

Psalm **22** *or* **139**
Genesis 42.29-end
Galatians 5.16-end

Genesis 42.29-end

'... they told him all that had happened to them' (v.29)

Over recent years, there has been much talk of an erosion of trust in many spheres of life from the national to the local. In times of anxiety and fear especially, people need people they can trust – relationships in which there is commitment to wellbeing and honest communication. In this ancient family saga, no one is handling anxiety well; honesty and trust are lacking.

Throughout chapter 42 of Genesis, the brothers have repeatedly described themselves as 'honest men', yet we, like Joseph, know this is not true. So today when we read that the brothers told their father '*all* that had happened' we know that this has not been their modus operandi in the past. There is also a hint in verse 36 that Jacob knows this, that he has never really trusted them ever since the day they returned without Joseph and presented him with a blood-stained robe implying Joseph had been killed by wild animals (Genesis 37). Perhaps even more darkly, Jacob cannot trust his sons because he knows how he dealt with his own brother Esau and deceived *his* father Isaac (Genesis 27).

It would be foolish to believe that all would suddenly be well if the brothers now truly told Jacob 'all' that had ever happened, but at least their decisions in a messy place would be lived in the light rather than trying to negotiate from the shadows. What might this mean for us today?

COLLECT

Almighty God,
whose Son Jesus Christ fasted forty days in the wilderness,
and was tempted as we are, yet without sin:
give us grace to discipline ourselves in obedience to your Spirit;
and, as you know our weakness,
so may we know your power to save;
through Jesus Christ your Son our Lord,
who is alive and reigns with you,
in the unity of the Holy Spirit,
one God, now and for ever.

Reflection by **Rachel Treweek**

Psalms 59, **63** *or* 120, **121**, 122
Genesis 43.1-15
Galatians 6

Saturday 12 March

Genesis 43.1-15

'... may God Almighty grant you mercy' (v.14)

A viral pandemic, like a time of famine, highlights the limits of our control, and at times in our lives we can feel helpless in the situations we find ourselves in. Furthermore, in our desire to be in control, we can sometimes be tempted to act in ways that are manipulative, deceitful or selfish. We have seen it all in this family story.

Yet, if the lies and deception so prevalent in the episodes thus far have left a bad taste in our mouths, there is now a sweetness emerging not only literally in the gifts of honey and nuts, but also metaphorically in the truth-telling we are now witnessing and the good desire for people's wellbeing expressed by both Jacob and Judah.

In this place of truth and love, we see an embracing of the present that is to be lived to the best of Jacob's ability and yet with a letting go and an acceptance that he is not in control. Whether the outcome is to be joy or pain, God will not abandon him.

Whether we are facing today with a sense of dread or joyful expectancy, how might we live the reality of today to our utmost best, entrusting ourselves and those we are concerned about to God whose love is unchanging and who will not abandon us?

Heavenly Father,
your Son battled with the powers of darkness,
and grew closer to you in the desert:
help us to use these days to grow in wisdom and prayer
that we may witness to your saving love
in Jesus Christ our Lord.

COLLECT

Monday 14 March

Genesis 43.16-end

'When Joseph came home...' (v.26)

In today's episode, there is much mention of the word 'house' – the place where Joseph dwells. This is where the brothers are invited to enter, and initially they do so with fear in their hearts. The steward reassures them, but they remain on edge as they await Joseph's return and the pending meal.

At this point the translation says that Joseph returned 'home' – a word that is subtly different from house and perhaps stands out because there is a question mark over whether Joseph is yet truly 'at home'. He is certainly not yet 'at home' with his family, and the pain of the separation from his brother Benjamin runs deep. Thankfully, the episode ends with anticipation that a home-coming is in sight. As the brothers eat from Joseph's table and are 'merry with him', there is a sense of being on the threshold of reconciliation, with the possibility of peace between them and within them.

The word 'homeless' is often used to describe someone who has no permanent building to inhabit, but it might be more accurate to use the word to describe a state of being. St Augustine of Hippo once wrote 'Thou hast made us for thyself O Lord, and our heart is restless until it finds its rest in thee.' Amid the activity of your life and the places you inhabit, how at home are you today?

COLLECT

Almighty God,
you show to those who are in error the light of your truth,
that they may return to the way of righteousness:
grant to all those who are admitted
    into the fellowship of Christ's religion,
that they may reject those things
    that are contrary to their profession,
and follow all such things as are agreeable to the same;
through our Lord Jesus Christ,
who is alive and reigns with you,
in the unity of the Holy Spirit,
one God, now and for ever.

Reflection by **Rachel Treweek**

Psalm **50** *or* **132**, 133
Genesis 44.1-17
Hebrews 2.1-9

Tuesday 15 March

Genesis 44.1-17

'What deed is this that you have done?' (v.15)

Being wrongfully accused is torturous where there is no one able to prove your innocence. Those who are accused are left utterly vulnerable and seemingly helpless. This is what we now see in this complex web of relationships among the brothers, and it is uncomfortable to watch.

We don't know whether Benjamin attempted to assure his brothers that he was innocent or whether the brothers' voicing of guilt is rooted in a genuine belief that Benjamin has somehow undermined them. Either way, there is something to be admired in the brothers' care for Benjamin, and it is important for Joseph to see this. Here are his brothers who are changed and who now wish to live in peace, although it is impossible for them to feel peaceful despite Joseph telling them to 'go up in peace.'

If, as Christ's followers, we wish to be people of peace, then we need to ask ourselves not only about how we speak up for those in our world today who are wrongfully accused and subjected to humiliation, but also how we support and care for those who are genuinely guilty of wrongdoing yet remain fellow human beings. It is an uncomfortable question; it raises numerous issues for us as individuals, communities and as society, but it is an appropriate question to ponder in Lent as we reflect on our own lives in a spirit of repentance and hope.

Almighty God,
by the prayer and discipline of Lent
may we enter into the mystery of Christ's sufferings,
and by following in his Way
come to share in his glory;
through Jesus Christ our Lord.

COLLECT

Reflection by **Rachel Treweek** | 19

Wednesday 16 March

Psalm **35** *or* **119.153-end**
Genesis 44.18-end
Hebrews 2.10-end

Genesis 44.18-end

'... please let your servant remain as a slave' (v.33)

Years earlier, in Genesis 37, it was Judah who proposed that they sell Joseph as a slave. There was no regard for the welfare of his brother or his father. Now it is Judah who boldly offers *himself* as a slave to ensure that his father and his brother Benjamin are honoured. Here is love, but we are unable to see Judah's heart and mind, and thus we cannot be sure of all that is driving him. Mingled with love there may also be guilt or pride or a fear of failure.

Our desire to grow in love of God, neighbour and self will rarely be free of the influence of our darker inner drivers, and so it is that the apostle Paul writing to the church in Philippi says: 'Do nothing from selfish ambition or conceit, but in humility regard others as better than yourselves. Let each of you look not to your own interests, but to the interests of others. Let the same mind be in you that was in Christ Jesus.' (Philippians 2.3-5)

Jesus Christ was motivated purely by love, and it was love alone that resulted in him emptying himself and taking the form of a slave (Philippians 2.7). For us, as followers of Christ, the days of Lent offer the opportunity to recognize our mixed motives more clearly and to open ourselves more fully to the unconditional love of God revealed in Christ.

COLLECT

Almighty God,
you show to those who are in error the light of your truth,
that they may return to the way of righteousness:
grant to all those who are admitted
    into the fellowship of Christ's religion,
that they may reject those things
    that are contrary to their profession,
and follow all such things as are agreeable to the same;
through our Lord Jesus Christ,
who is alive and reigns with you,
in the unity of the Holy Spirit,
one God, now and for ever.

20 | *Reflection by* **Rachel Treweek**

Psalm **34** *or* **143**, 146
Genesis 45.1-15
Hebrews 3.1-6

Thursday 17 March

Genesis 45.1-15

'And he kissed all his brothers and wept upon them ...' (v.15)

In today's episode, there is revelation and resolution. Yet perhaps it is surprising that that the brothers respond with such grace and appear to show no resentment. After all, once again Joseph has acted with superiority and power not unlike those years before when he taunted them with his dreams, which of course have now come true. Joseph has put his brothers through the wringer, yet perhaps there is a sense of having been absolved from their own game-playing all those years ago when they sold Joseph into slavery and deceived their father. We can only speculate as to the content of their conversation when they finally talked with each other.

For both Joseph and the brothers, there must be a sense of relief that all has been brought into the light. It is that crossroads described in Psalm 85.10 and translated so poignantly in the Authorized Version: 'Mercy and truth are met together, righteousness and peace have kissed each other.'

Lent is a good time to examine ourselves and name those places in our lives where there is a need for revelation and resolution, those places where the hiding or the pretence needs to stop and the truth be named. Sometimes, it is about putting something down or letting something go. The relief that will follow will be accompanied by all sorts of thoughts and emotions, but the good news is that God's work of healing can unfold.

COLLECT

Almighty God,
by the prayer and discipline of Lent
may we enter into the mystery of Christ's sufferings,
and by following in his Way
come to share in his glory;
through Jesus Christ our Lord.

Reflection by **Rachel Treweek** | 21

Friday 18 March

Genesis 45.16-end

'He was stunned; he could not believe them' (v. 26)

All the fear, sadness and loss in the family's story is now met with abundance and joy. There is almost a sense of 'happy ever after', yet the source of the happiness is not in the giving of the multiplicity of goods but rather in love and restored relationship.

Many years previously, Jacob too had proffered a lavish gift of material goods to family, although this time in fear (Genesis 33). He had gone to meet his estranged brother Esau and hoped that the numerous herds and flocks would be a gift to appease his brother whom he had wronged. However, Esau wanted none of it. The desired gift was that of reconciliation, and when Esau embraced Jacob, it seemed too good to be true, and he exclaimed that it was as if he had seen the face of God. There are resonances of that time of grace as Jacob now hears that Joseph is alive, and the brothers discover forgiveness and new possibility.

In these days of Lent, as we stumble towards Good Friday with all our struggles and flaws, the abundant treasure of Easter Day is still present. God is making all things new, and yet it is only by opening ourselves to the undeserved gift of God's overwhelming and abundant love that we will discover the gift of restoration and the 'happy ever after' that will one day be made complete.

COLLECT

Almighty God,
you show to those who are in error the light of your truth,
that they may return to the way of righteousness:
grant to all those who are admitted
    into the fellowship of Christ's religion,
that they may reject those things
    that are contrary to their profession,
and follow all such things as are agreeable to the same;
through our Lord Jesus Christ,
who is alive and reigns with you,
in the unity of the Holy Spirit,
one God, now and for ever.

Reflection by **Rachel Treweek**

Lent

Psalms 25, 147.1-12
Isaiah 11.1-10
Matthew 13.54-end

Saturday 19 March
Joseph of Nazareth

Matthew 13.54-end

'Is not this the carpenter's son?' (v.55)

Too often, we make assumptions about people based on what we know or have been told. Here, the people are blinded by their assumptions about Jesus, not least that he is the son of Joseph the carpenter.

We know very little about *this* Joseph, but we do know that he acted radically in not abandoning Mary. Any man betrothed to a woman who was found to be pregnant would usually have ensured she was publicly disgraced and probably stoned. What life had been like for Joseph and Mary as their young family grew up surrounded by rumour, we can only begin to imagine.

Yet it is not only Jesus' family who were potentially diminished by their community's assumptions; it was also the people themselves. They could have received so much blessing from opening their eyes and ears to the good news of Jesus Christ among them and allowed their astonishment to lead them to new discovery about God and themselves. Instead, their small-mindedness prevented them from tasting life in all its fullness.

Today is a good day to be aware of assumptions we may have of particular individuals around us that may prevent us from encountering God at work in them and through them. It may also be a day to challenge some of the assumptions we have about ourselves, a day to be expectant about what Christ can do in us and through us by the power of the Holy Spirit.

COLLECT

God our Father,
who from the family of your servant David
raised up Joseph the carpenter
to be the guardian of your incarnate Son
and husband of the Blessed Virgin Mary:
give us grace to follow him
in faithful obedience to your commands;
through Jesus Christ your Son our Lord,
who is alive and reigns with you,
in the unity of the Holy Spirit,
one God, now and for ever.

Reflection by **Rachel Treweek**

23

Monday 21 March

Psalms **5**, **7** or **1**, **2**, **3**
Genesis 47.1-27
Hebrews 4.14 – 5.10

Genesis 47.1-27

'… few and hard have been the years of my life' (v.9)

Today's reading foreshadows the history of redemption. It first has Jacob's family migrating to Egypt and coming under Pharaoh's protection. It then has Joseph enslaving the entire population of Egypt as famine engulfs the land. So Israel goes down into Egypt and yet, in the person of Joseph, prevails over the Egyptians. But that victory is here only prefigured. (It may also make us morally squeamish.) The true victory will come with Moses and the Exodus.

At the heart of faith is a story of slavery and freedom. Human experience is a struggle for survival, and nature is not benign, as the famine in Egypt demonstrates. We are all limited by forces beyond ourselves and have to seek to make the best of our few years on earth. However good our intentions may be, our actions have unforeseen consequences. There were good reasons for Jacob's family to migrate to Goshen, but we already know they will end up enslaved and oppressed.

We should consider today how far we have participated in the oppression of others through ignorance, weakness and our own deliberate fault. We should also reflect on any oppressions we have internalized, to our own and others' harm.

What talents and skills do we bring to the wellbeing of those around us and to their flourishing and freedom?

COLLECT

Almighty God,
whose most dear Son went not up to joy
    but first he suffered pain,
and entered not into glory before he was crucified:
mercifully grant that we, walking in the way of the cross,
may find it none other than the way of life and peace;
through Jesus Christ your Son our Lord,
who is alive and reigns with you,
in the unity of the Holy Spirit,
one God, now and for ever.

Reflection by **Angela Tilby**

Tuesday 22 March

Genesis 47.28 – end of 48

'God Almighty appeared to me ... in the land of Canaan' (48.3)

The story of Jacob's blessing of Joseph's sons has some confusing features, but we can discern a repeat of the pattern that has already emerged in earlier stories about Jacob. Jacob adopts Joseph's two sons, giving them a place within the tribes of Israel. But then, just as Jacob, the younger son, was preferred over the older son, Esau, so Joseph's younger son, Ephraim, is preferred over Manasseh.

Scripture is full of these jarring moments, and they point to the activities of a God who constantly points beyond human preference and tradition in enacting salvation. God will not be confined to human rules and traditions, no matter how time-honoured and respected they are.

Today's reading also has Jacob pleading to be buried in Bethlehem, in the land of Canaan where his beloved wife Rachel died. Before he makes this request, he tells Joseph of his encounter with God at Haran (Genesis 28.10-32) in the vision of the heavenly staircase and the angels. God does not forget us in old age, as we draw near to death. It is often here that the meaning of our lives is revealed to us and passed on to the next generation.

In a society that often seems to find death unacceptable, how do we prepare for a good death?

Eternal God,
give us insight
to discern your will for us,
to give up what harms us,
and to seek the perfection we are promised
in Jesus Christ our Lord.

COLLECT

Wednesday 23 March

Psalm **38** *or* 119.1-32
Genesis 49.1-32
Hebrews 6.13-end

Genesis 49.1-32

'The sceptre shall not depart from Judah ...' (v.10)

Jacob's dying wish is to preserve continuity, and so preserve the promise of God to his descendants. Jacob's last words are a series of predictions about the character and fate of the twelve tribes. As one who has shown in his lifetime a blend of faithfulness and deceit, Jacob has some penetrating insights into the characters of his progeny. They will not all enjoy a happy and prosperous future. As with any family, some members will bring glory to the family name while others bring shame.

The Bible does not idealize the chosen people. The twelve tribes are not exceptional; their legacy is as full of human violence and error as it is of obedience and blessing. The tribe of Judah will carry on the faith of Israel into the future. This is a hint of the Messiah's future reign.

During Lent, it is worth reflecting on our own family history and on what we have inherited for good or ill. Is there a patriarchal or matriarchal figure who looms large in family history? And has their effect been benign or destructive?

Jacob's predictions are his blessings. Whether for good or ill, he cares for his sons individually. Our family and tribal identity may be important, but God knows us intimately, by name.

COLLECT

Almighty God,
whose most dear Son went not up to joy
    but first he suffered pain,
and entered not into glory before he was crucified:
mercifully grant that we, walking in the way of the cross,
may find it none other than the way of life and peace;
through Jesus Christ your Son our Lord,
who is alive and reigns with you,
in the unity of the Holy Spirit,
one God, now and for ever.

Reflection by **Angela Tilby**

Psalms **56**, 57 *or* 14, **15**, 16
Genesis 49.33 – end of 50
Hebrews 7.1-10

Thursday 24 March

Genesis 49.33 – end of 50

*'... though you intended to do harm to me, God intended it
for good' (v.20)*

After a significant death there are often complicated family
emotions to be played out. The death of Jacob is no exception. In
spite of the years they have been settled in the land of Goshen,
Joseph's brothers are still plagued with guilt going back to their
original plot to kill him, and then, when this was foiled, their casual
selling of him into slavery (chapter 37). Guilt is not easily admitted,
and the brothers make up a story suggesting Jacob has begged him
to forgive them. When Joseph weeps, it is not clear whether he is
moved by his father's supposed plea or by his brothers' continued
deceit.

In the end it doesn't matter. When there is a heart to forgive, simple
contrition is enough. A clinical reckoning of wrongs is beside the
point as the currency of forgiveness is new life, not point scoring.
Joseph's willingness to forgive his brothers is enough, and he readily
provides for their continuity and wellbeing.

Lent is a season of repentance and forgiveness. Are there ancient
family wrongs in our lives waiting to be forgiven? What steps can
we take to acknowledge them and put them right? The opportunity
will not be there for ever. But if we take the time at least to
acknowledge what is wrong, we may find liberation and blessing.

Eternal God,
give us insight
to discern your will for us,
to give up what harms us,
and to seek the perfection we are promised
in Jesus Christ our Lord.

COLLECT

Reflection by **Angela Tilby** | 27

Friday 25 March

Annunciation of Our Lord
to the Blessed Virgin Mary

1 Samuel 2.1-10

'The Lord ... brings low, he also exalts' (v.7)

Today's reading is chosen for the Feast of the Annunciation. Hannah, the once barren wife of Elkanah, has prayed for a child and her prayer has been answered. Her little son's name, Samuel, means 'asked of the Lord'. Her song of triumph prefigures Mary's Magnificat (Luke 1.46-55), introducing phrases that are almost identical to that of Mary's song.

There are major differences, however. Hannah had pleaded with God for a child; Mary was not expecting the angel's call and was troubled by it. Hannah's response was unambiguous joy; Mary, 'with child from the Holy Spirit', faced the possibility of shame and exclusion. But in spite of these differences, the Song of Hannah and the Song of Mary express a similar response of sheer delight in God's readiness to hear the cry of the poor and humble.

Prayer begins in a recognition of our need of God. We come to God not in the strength of our achievements, but in our littleness and insignificance. However important our daily work, however necessary we are to those around us, there is a part of us that is empty, needy, small in every sense. That is where God's Spirit prays in us and where God comes to make his home in us, and where our lives become truly fruitful. Rejoice in God your Saviour!

COLLECT

We beseech you, O Lord,
pour your grace into our hearts,
that as we have known the incarnation of your Son Jesus Christ
   by the message of an angel,
so by his cross and passion
we may be brought to the glory of his resurrection;
through Jesus Christ your Son our Lord,
who is alive and reigns with you,
in the unity of the Holy Spirit,
one God, now and for ever.

Reflection by **Angela Tilby**

Psalm **31** *or* 20, 21, **23**
Exodus 1.22 – 2.10
Hebrews 8

Exodus 1.22 – 2.10

'I drew him out of the water' (v.10)

It is appropriate to read from the book of Exodus in the weeks before Easter. In the cycle of the Christian year, we are being brought to encounter the dark side of our nature, our captivity to habits and limitations we have imposed on ourselves and which others have imposed on us.

So we read of the Hebrew people in captivity in Egypt. Any newborn male offspring is under sentence of death. The preservation of the baby Moses is orchestrated by women: his mother and sister, the daughter of Pharaoh and her attendants. There is nothing obviously miraculous about the protection given to Moses. It comes about as a result of cunning, watchfulness, kindness and care.

Moses stands here for the future of God's people and for hope. We know that Moses will grow up to become Israel's saviour and deliverer. But at this stage he is helpless. His future depends on the faithfulness of those who simply will not let him die, who in the midst of deep oppression and violence, choose life.

This fundamental choice of life is significant for all of us. What today would we guard at all costs, refuse to let go of, protect and preserve against all adversaries? Our answer may tell us something about where our true vocation lies and what we should concentrate on in our work and leisure this weekend.

Eternal God,
give us insight
to discern your will for us,
to give up what harms us,
and to seek the perfection we are promised
in Jesus Christ our Lord.

COLLECT

Reflection by **Angela Tilby** | 29

Monday 28 March

Psalms 70, **77** *or* 27, **30**
Exodus 2.11-22
Hebrews 9.1-14

Exodus 2.11-22

'I have been an alien residing in a foreign land' (v. 22)

It is not clear from today's reading how Moses came to understand that he was the child of a slave race and not an Egyptian prince. It can be assumed that his mother must have told him, but he was still brought up as the son of Pharaoh's daughter.

In the New Testament, Moses' identification with his suffering people is seen as an archetype of what it means to suffer for Christ (Hebrews 11.23-26). Yet this was not a choice so much as a revelation. It is the casual beating up of a Hebrew slave by an Egyptian overseer that brings Moses, violently, to an awareness of his true identity. By killing the Egyptian, he discovered who he was. Yet coming to terms with this was not easy. Even after he had fled from Egypt, the daughters of the priest of Midian made the assumption that he was an Egyptian.

This passage is a reminder that Christian vocation often begins in a murky place, and it is sometimes brought into focus through threat and disaster. The birth of Moses' son suggests that it took time for him to recognize that he had a task ahead. He has been alien in two senses, both in Egypt as a Hebrew and from Egypt during his time in Midian. The wake-up call is at hand.

COLLECT

Merciful Lord,
absolve your people from their offences,
that through your bountiful goodness
we may all be delivered from the chains of those sins
which by our frailty we have committed;
grant this, heavenly Father,
for Jesus Christ's sake, our blessed Lord and Saviour,
who is alive and reigns with you,
in the unity of the Holy Spirit,
one God, now and for ever.

Reflection by **Angela Tilby**

Exodus 2.23 – 3.20

'And he said, "Here I am."' (3.4)

This is one of the most extraordinary and powerful passages of Scripture. God's disclosure to Moses of his true name and his saving intention is fundamental to both Jewish and Christian faith. Historically, this is often considered to be the original moment of divine revelation, pre-dating the patriarchal stories that have come down to us more in the form of saga or myth than history.

The core of it is that God is mystery. No one knows precisely what the Hebrew consonants of his name mean, and in Jewish tradition, the name must never be vocalized. God is ultimately free and sovereign. We cannot control or contain God. Yet this mysterious 'I am' chooses to liberate his people and to make Moses the agent of his deliverance.

Our Christian identity is bound up with our personal relationship with God. The God who is mystery, whose name cannot be spoken, addresses us by name, knowing us far more deeply than we can ever know ourselves and seeing potential in us that is far different from what we might imagine. Moses is not everyone's idea of a hero. He is full of doubt and questioning, fully aware of his past, exiled even from his place of exile. He is simply not the stuff leaders are made of. And yet ...

What resonances are there here with your own experience of Christian call and obedience?

COLLECT

Merciful Lord,
you know our struggle to serve you:
when sin spoils our lives
and overshadows our hearts,
come to our aid
and turn us back to you again;
through Jesus Christ our Lord.

Reflection by **Angela Tilby**   31

Wednesday 30 March

Psalms 63, **90** *or* **34**
Exodus 4.1-23
Hebrews 10.1-18

Exodus 4.1-23

'I will be with your mouth and teach you what you are to speak'
(v.12)

Moses needs to be prepared for the task ahead. He has to be trained for the job, and God is presented here as his 'personal trainer' in a series of exercises that are both physically and mentally demanding.

What the training reveals is Moses' insecurity. The miracles of the staff and of the sudden leprosy suggest Moses has to understand both his fear and his inner violence. His stammer makes him unfit in his own eyes to be God's messenger to Pharaoh. God engages with Moses angrily, and yet the anger gives way to care and a readiness to compromise. Having Aaron as a mouthpiece will not be an unmixed blessing to Moses (think ahead to the incident of the Golden Calf in chapter 32!), but for now God is prepared for Moses to have a representative to speak his words.

God's training comes with a warning: Pharaoh will not listen to Moses' request to let the people go. The story that follows is one of persistence and determination. Moses has to learn as he goes along. He does not have natural gifts of confidence or charisma. Yet as he takes the first step of obedience in leaving Midian, he is learning to trust his divine trainer.

COLLECT

Merciful Lord,
absolve your people from their offences,
that through your bountiful goodness
we may all be delivered from the chains of those sins
which by our frailty we have committed;
grant this, heavenly Father,
for Jesus Christ's sake, our blessed Lord and Saviour,
who is alive and reigns with you,
in the unity of the Holy Spirit,
one God, now and for ever.

| *Reflection by* **Angela Tilby**

Psalms 53, **86** *or* 37*
Exodus 4.27 – 6.1
Hebrews 10.19-25

Thursday 31 March

Exodus 4.27 – 6.1

'... by a mighty hand he will let them go' (6.1)

So, at the time of year when we are trudging through Lent, we begin to read the saga of Israel's deliverance from salvery, a foreshadowing of our deliverance from sin and death at Easter. The struggle for freedom is a long one. Pharaoh justifies his oppression by insisting that he 'does not know the Lord' and therefore has no responsibility towards his people.

We recognize here the strategy of present-day tyrants who stir up resentment against hard-pressed minorities. Again, like demagogues of our own time, Pharaoh secretly fears the people he is oppressing and calculates that they will be more effectively subdued if their task is made impossible. This sparks further protest, which, in turn, deepens the oppression. Inevitably, the people turn on Moses and Aaron who have raised their hopes in vain. Never a natural leader, Moses has little resilience when he meets opposition, and he turns to God in complaint. God's response is to reassert his promise: Pharaoh will let the people go.

The Exodus story has inspired protest movements in our own time. It gives a model of how oppressed people come to understand their own oppression and challenge it. This requires both courage and faith. The oppressor is never as strong as he appears.

What are the obstacles that we face that seem immovable, the forces that restrict our freedom in Christ?

Merciful Lord,
you know our struggle to serve you:
when sin spoils our lives
and overshadows our hearts,
come to our aid
and turn us back to you again;
through Jesus Christ our Lord.

COLLECT

Reflection by **Angela Tilby** | 33

Friday I April

Psalms **102** *or* **31**
Exodus 6.2-13
Hebrews 10.26-end

Exodus 6.2-13

'I will take you as my people, and I will be your God' (v.7)

This chapter begins a new phase in God's relationship with his captive people as God promises to draw them into a personal covenant with himself and give them the land promised to the patriarchs. This is God's sovereign choice and will eventually be enacted at Sinai after the escape from Egypt.

It is poignantly sad that this sign of favour is not received by the people. They are simply too broken to listen. When God instructs Moses to approach Pharaoh again with the demand to let his people go, Moses is reluctant and even seems to blame himself for the people's indifference to God's promise.

When life is strained by suffering or injustice it becomes impossible to hear news of hope. It is almost easier to plod on in despair than to be open to what might turn out to be another disappointment.

The Christian life does not guarantee that we shall not at times be overwhelmed. What it does guarantee is that God does not reject us or forget us. Even as the people are languishing in misery, Moses and Aaron are being trained for their next confrontation with Pharaoh. The powers of darkness are sometimes overwhelming, but even they will eventually yield to the truth and mercy of God.

COLLECT

Merciful Lord,
absolve your people from their offences,
that through your bountiful goodness
we may all be delivered from the chains of those sins
which by our frailty we have committed;
grant this, heavenly Father,
for Jesus Christ's sake, our blessed Lord and Saviour,
who is alive and reigns with you,
in the unity of the Holy Spirit,
one God, now and for ever.

Reflection by **Angela Tilby**

Psalm **32** *or* 41, **42**, **43**
Exodus 7.8-end
Hebrews 11.1-16

Saturday 2 April

Exodus 7.8-end

'By this you shall know that I am the Lord' (v.17)

The long process of wearing down Pharaoh's resistance begins. God demonstrates through Moses and Aaron that his divine powers over life and death are greater than anything Pharaoh can imitate, although he and his magicians will try their best. Moses' turning of the river water to blood was a strike at the heart of Pharaoh's power and prosperity, for the fertility of the land depended entirely on the great River Nile.

Pharaoh's indifference even to his own people's welfare is revealed by the imitative tricks of his own sorcerors. He wants to demonstrate his strength and simply doesn't care that his people are left scrabbling for water.

What is being shown is the fragility of those who claim to be all-powerful. Narcissistic egoism eventually undermines itself. When we find ourselves up against authority that is all about ego, we need to remember that the appearance of strength often masks inner weakness. If you know your weakness and depend on God, you will ultimately prevail.

How does this affect your prayer today, especially for those who wield power? How would you pray for those who are mistreated by irresponsible leaders? And how might you demonstrate the power made perfect in our human weakness for the sake of those who are unjustly oppressed?

COLLECT

Merciful Lord,
you know our struggle to serve you:
when sin spoils our lives
and overshadows our hearts,
come to our aid
and turn us back to you again;
through Jesus Christ our Lord.

Reflection by **Angela Tilby** | 35

Monday 4 April

Psalms **73**, 121 *or* **44**
Exodus 8.1-19
Hebrews 11.17-31

Exodus 8.1-19

*'If you refuse to let them go, I will plague your whole country
with frogs' (v.2)*

This is glorious knockabout stuff. There's a goody (Moses) and a
baddy (Pharaoh), and in the struggle to see who wins, the goody has
the advantage of having incredible magic powers, whereas the
baddy has the upper hand because he's the boss. The irony, of course,
is that we know who is going to win in the end – and it's not the
boss.

So, how can we imaginatively enter this story? Perhaps in the way it
was originally intended, as a tall story, to be told in a darkened room
late at night with firelight flickering on the walls – as a 'Once upon
a time' story, a fairy tale.

Or, maybe we can enter it, as might also have been intended, as a
saga. Sagas need to be told where lots of people gather to listen to
a storyteller who, with sweeping gestures and a thunderous voice,
enraptures us with the rhythm of the narrative. We are taken out of
the here-and-now and transported to a world of danger and delight.

But suppose that a truth is lurking in the story-saga and in the fairy
tale: a truth about God. Could it be that at the heart of all great
stories lies the Original Story? The Word behind and within the
words – words that, like the most haunting music, lift us into a new
place and help us to see, even if only for a moment, the power and
majesty and infinite possibility of God.

COLLECT

Most merciful God,
who by the death and resurrection of your Son Jesus Christ
delivered and saved the world:
grant that by faith in him who suffered on the cross
we may triumph in the power of his victory;
through Jesus Christ your Son our Lord,
who is alive and reigns with you,
in the unity of the Holy Spirit,
one God, now and for ever.

Reflection by **Christopher Herbert**

Psalms **35**, 123 *or* **48**, 52
Exodus 8.20-end
Hebrews 11.32 – 12.2

Tuesday 5 April

Exodus 8.20-end

'Then the Lord said to Moses, "Rise early in the morning and present yourself before Pharaoh"' (v.20)

Political subtlety now enters the story. Moses waylays Pharaoh as he is going down to the river. In the world of the media, ambushing your victim to get an interview is known as 'door-stepping'; anyone who has been on the receiving end of it will know how irritating and threatening it can be. Moses is being ruthlessly crafty.

But a night passes – filled with the tormenting buzzing of flies. Pharaoh thinks things through and knows that he must get the upper hand again. So, he summons Moses and Aaron and offers them a deal: to go into the wilderness to make a sacrifice, on condition that they must return.

Politically, it's risky. What if Moses and Aaron and their followers don't come back? Pharaoh weighs it up and decides the risk is worth taking. Fortunately, Moses, Aaron and their people keep their promise and return. Pharaoh is back on top, except, of course, as we know, he isn't.

This is a story that subtly twists and turns. No doubt the actions of Moses, as presented by the author, are designed to be emulated. It calls to mind Jesus' injunction about being wise as serpents and innocent as doves.

So, now recall any negotiations you have ever been involved in. Would you class yourself as astute, like the serpent, or innocent, like the dove? But perhaps our task is not to be either like the serpent or like the dove, rather to be both.

Gracious Father,
you gave up your Son
out of love for the world:
lead us to ponder the mysteries of his passion,
that we may know eternal peace
through the shedding of our Saviour's blood,
Jesus Christ our Lord.

COLLECT

Reflection by **Christopher Herbert**   37

Wednesday 6 April

Exodus 9.1-12

'Then the Lord said ... "Take handfuls of soot from the kiln"' (v.8)

Here comes divine retribution: a pandemic caused by something as simple as soot from a chimney...

If this were a fairy story, the morality would not matter, because justice and goodness would win in the end. But if we see the story from the point of view of the Egyptians, it becomes horrific and completely unjust. This god, the god of Moses, is apparently all-powerful but is also entirely amoral. Pharaoh is being obdurate and is made so because the Lord (note this) has created him that way. And, because Pharaoh won't give in, everyone gets it in the neck, literally with a plague of boils. This painful, inflammatory skin condition miraculously does not affect Moses and his people but invades everyone in the host community.

It is not the fantastical content of the story that is bothersome – one can cope with that; it's the implied theology that is so impossible. Let's get this straight. Our moral outrage consists of two things: first, the gross injustice of the entire population of Egypt suffering, and second, the Lord himself deliberately causing Pharaoh to be obtuse by 'hardening his heart'. In our terms, therefore, it is the Lord who is morally culpable.

No amount of casuistry will prevent us seeing this. This leaves us in a deep quandary. If we cannot tolerate such unjust behaviour, even in a story, what can we do about it, apart from just noting the fact? The answer lies in Christ, in whom the true justice at the heart of God was revealed.

COLLECT

Most merciful God,
who by the death and resurrection of your Son Jesus Christ
delivered and saved the world:
grant that by faith in him who suffered on the cross
we may triumph in the power of his victory;
through Jesus Christ your Son our Lord,
who is alive and reigns with you,
in the unity of the Holy Spirit,
one God, now and for ever.

| *Reflection by* **Christopher Herbert**

Psalms **40**, 125 *or* 56, **57** (63*)
Exodus 9.13-end
Hebrews 12.14-end

Thursday 7 April

Exodus 9.13-end

'Those officials of Pharaoh who feared the word of the Lord hurried their slaves and livestock off to a secure place' (v.20)

And now there is dissension in the Egyptian court. Some believe very readily in the threats being made by Moses; others take no notice. There's no longer a common front, and with division comes the faint possibility, from Moses' point of view, of success. But it is not just the success of leading his people out of slavery, it is a theological victory that is almost within sight.

You will have noticed that when Moses addresses Pharaoh, he refers to his message of liberation as one he has been given by the 'God of the Hebrews'. In a country with many gods – including Amun, the king of the gods, and Isis, the protector goddess – the God of the Hebrews would have been regarded as a little, local, tribal deity. Nothing to worry about. However, the message from Moses is that the God of the Hebrews is like no other: '... there is no one like me in all the earth'.

This is a titanic struggle. It is not just about the freedom of the Hebrew slaves but is also about the very nature of the Divine. Preposterous as it must have sounded, the argument is that what others might regard as a tiny, unimportant god, is actually the God above all gods, the Creator of the Universe, the one who has chosen a slave-people to be the carriers of his Name for evermore.

It is worth considering, therefore, whether our own concept of God is too small.

COLLECT

Gracious Father,
you gave up your Son
out of love for the world:
lead us to ponder the mysteries of his passion,
that we may know eternal peace
through the shedding of our Saviour's blood,
Jesus Christ our Lord.

Reflection by **Christopher Herbert** | 39

Friday 8 April

Psalms **22**, 126 *or* **51**, 54
Exodus 10
Hebrews 13.1-16

Exodus 10

'... a darkness that can be felt' (v.21)

Sometimes, in sagas that have been written by many authors, as the plague stories appear to have been, there is a flash of poetry. So it is in today's reading with the phrase 'a darkness that can be felt'. It is difficult in our overlit, urbanized world to experience real darkness, but if you have been caving, you will know that when you turn off your helmet-light deep underground, the darkness is total. Even so, disorientating though the experience is, it is not a darkness that can be 'felt'. The darkness of a cave is thinner than that.

But a darkness that can be felt is a different matter. It is the darkness of nightmares. The darkness that has an inchoate shape. The darkness in the depths of our being. It was perhaps a darkness of soul containing intense uncertainty that was beginning to trouble Pharaoh. He starts to shout and threaten.

The long drama of the plagues is obviously moving to a climax. The two adversaries have been battling with each other for some time, and only with an assertion of naked power can Pharaoh retain control.

For those of us who try to follow Christ, there are also moments of deep darkness – an emptiness, a barrenness of soul, an absence that is like a presence. Unable to feel our way forward, we are reduced to doing nothing. Kneeling in a darkness so dense it can be felt, all we can do is to await the light of grace.

COLLECT

Most merciful God,
who by the death and resurrection of your Son Jesus Christ
delivered and saved the world:
grant that by faith in him who suffered on the cross
we may triumph in the power of his victory;
through Jesus Christ your Son our Lord,
who is alive and reigns with you,
in the unity of the Holy Spirit,
one God, now and for ever.

Reflection by **Christopher Herbert**

Psalms **23**, 127 *or* **68**
Exodus 11
Hebrews 13.17-end

Saturday 9 April

Exodus 11

*'... so that you may know that the Lord makes a distinction
between Egypt and Israel' (v.7)*

It is a question about choice. If you believe that God chose the people
of Israel and established a special and everlasting covenant with
them, then this story fits into that overarching narrative. But
remember that this is a story. It is not history. It is not journalistic
reportage. It is a story written down many centuries after the events
it purports to describe.

So why was it written when it was written? Some scholars argue that
the stories of Moses represent an ancient oral tradition; they point
out that the name 'Moses' is very like other Egyptian names. Others
argue that the various author-editors of the book of Exodus adapted
those oral traditions and, in the eighth century BC, or maybe even
later, wove them into a coherent narrative about Israel's early origins.
Perhaps they did this at a time when Israel felt it was under external
military threat, a time when God's special relationship with a
legendary hero might have had a morale-boosting contemporary
relevance. We cannot be sure.

What is abundantly clear is that it is a story both about the almighty
power of the Divine and also about the choice of a special people.
Nothing and no one, not even a Pharaoh, can get in the way of that
special covenantal relationship.

So, suppose that, through Jesus, God has extended that original
covenant. Does God continue to call and challenge people? Can we
stand in the way of that call? How shall we respond?

COLLECT

Gracious Father,
you gave up your Son
out of love for the world:
lead us to ponder the mysteries of his passion,
that we may know eternal peace
through the shedding of our Saviour's blood,
Jesus Christ our Lord.

Reflection by **Christopher Herbert**

41

Monday 11 April

Monday of Holy Week

Lamentations 1.1-12*a*

'Look and see if there is any sorrow like my sorrow' (v.12)

The picture that today's reading presents is not just about abandoned streets and closed shops. There is more going on than a lockdown. Jerusalem after its people have been deported by the Babylonians is left violated, humiliated: the shocking image is of a woman who has been raped by enemy soldiers, left in torn clothes, sobbing with pain and terror.

The harrowing poems that make up the book of Lamentations convey the sense of disbelieving horror that must have overwhelmed those who witnessed the city's capture and the brutal expulsion of its people. It highlights the question: 'Is God to be trusted?'

The Holy Week journey begins uncompromisingly with the moment when the answer seems to be 'No'. It prompts us to think not just about human suffering in general, but about that very specific kind of suffering that has to do with betrayal and desertion. 'Look and see', insists the poet: don't look away, don't make light of this cry from the depths.

But we need to remember: *this is the Word of the Lord*. The anguished crying of those who are betrayed and believe they are forgotten, unseen and unheard, becomes God's call to us – so that the terrible betrayal and abuse of human beings is not God's betrayal of us but ours of God. Refusing to 'look and see', to acknowledge the pain of those doubly betrayed by being hurt *and* being silenced, is turning from God. Hard as it is, looking honestly at this is a turning to him; a conversion.

COLLECT

Almighty and everlasting God,
who in your tender love towards the human race
    sent your Son our Saviour Jesus Christ
to take upon him our flesh
and to suffer death upon the cross:
grant that we may follow the example of his patience and humility,
and also be made partakers of his resurrection;
through Jesus Christ your Son our Lord,
who is alive and reigns with you,
in the unity of the Holy Spirit,
one God, now and for ever.

Reflection by **Rowan Williams**

Psalm 27
Lamentations 3.1-18
Luke 22. [24-38] 39-53

Tuesday 12 April
Tuesday of Holy Week

Lamentations 3.1-18
'... he has made me dwell in darkness' (v.6, RSV)

It feels sometimes as though God is the real enemy. He has lured us into trusting in him, and now our confidence is shown to be empty. The poet's mind and heart are described as if they were a city under siege, a soldier under fire. He is exposed to the derision of those who never took the risk of faith in the first place.

As the chapter unfolds, the poet's voice shifts bit by bit. He has been silenced – not by human indifference and cruelty, like the tragic voice we heard in the first chapter, but by the sheer impossibility of making anything melodious and eloquent out of the world as it really is.

Patience: don't think you have a formula that will make it all easier. Sit with the reality of this pain and chaos beyond your control. Don't tidy it up to suit yourself.

Perhaps all you're left with is hope. And perhaps the readiness to stay and not turn away or tidy up hints at how we could think of God himself. It is not at all that he has set out to inflict pain; but in a world where pain happens, he is never pushed out or immobilised.

To come anywhere near grasping this, we have to let go of any confidence that we can make satisfying sense of things by our own effort and ingenuity. We must share the loss and disorientation of the most vulnerable – the cities under siege, the soldiers under fire. Silence; but a knowledge – *in* the silence – of something not defeated.

COLLECT

True and humble king,
hailed by the crowd as Messiah:
grant us the faith to know you and love you,
that we may be found beside you
on the way of the cross,
which is the path of glory.

Reflection by **Rowan Williams** | 43

Wednesday 13 April
Wednesday of Holy Week

Psalm 102 [*or* 102.1-18]
Wisdom 1.16 – 2.1; 2.12-22
or Jeremiah 11.18-20
Luke 22.54-end

Jeremiah 11.18-20
'... that his name will no longer be remembered!' (v.19)

The prophet's enemies want to make sure that he is not *remembered*. The fact that he spoke of judgement and hope, that he named the wounds and the violence and the urgent summons of God in the midst of it all – this must be forgotten. There is not really that much wrong with the world – or if there is, it is someone else's problem, someone else's business. And the crying of the violated and abused is at worst a matter of sad 'noises off', not the word of the Lord.

The prophet walks into the trap. He has no strategy or defence but the truth of what he sees and hears, what has been shown him. He is not there to advance a theory, but to witness to the God whose silent working in the heart of things never disappears. So the prophet's guileless simplicity of response puts him at mortal risk.

Yet it is only his simple wholeness of seeing and hearing that makes him a true prophet. If he wraps it up with his own agenda and his own security, he stops showing the truth in its nakedness. His witness would come and go like that of others.

But it's because he is exposed to God, fearlessly open to God, that what he says and what he shows can't be forgotten, whether he lives or dies. He has bound himself to the truth; and the living truth binds itself to him, and makes his memory live and his words keep on piercing the heart.

COLLECT

Almighty and everlasting God,
who in your tender love towards the human race
    sent your Son our Saviour Jesus Christ
to take upon him our flesh
and to suffer death upon the cross:
grant that we may follow the example of his patience and humility,
and also be made partakers of his resurrection;
through Jesus Christ your Son our Lord,
who is alive and reigns with you,
in the unity of the Holy Spirit,
one God, now and for ever.

| *Reflection by* **Rowan Williams**

Psalms 42, 43
Leviticus 16.2-24
Luke 23.1-25

Thursday 14 April
Maundy Thursday

Leviticus 16.2-24

'He shall ... send him away into the wilderness' (v.21, RSV)

The strange and haunting ritual described seems at first sight to suggest that for things to be healed and renewed, the past has to be sent away. The scapegoat carries the people's sins out of sight, into the remote desert.

But this does not mean that the past is just obliterated. This is a ritual of *healing*. Before the goat is sent away, the priest has recited over its head the record of failure and injury and rebellion. We're not told to forget, but to remember in a way that makes us able to be free. Our sins and our wounds are named, not ignored, as we saw yesterday with the words of the prophet; and then they are set in the context where they can be healed.

In Hebrew Scripture, the desert is the place where God's people can begin again, where the familiar protections are taken away so that God's call can be heard. So the scapegoat takes into that empty and comfortless place all the memories of hurts given and received, of anger, fear, rejection. In the harsh light of the desert, these things are stripped bare to the life and love of God. In this light we can see the true weight and cost of saying no to God and each other. And we remember the God whose purpose is atonement, making us 'at one' both with the divine life and with the life of the world we share.

'Do this in remembrance.' Be at one, in service and communion.

> True and humble king,
> hailed by the crowd as Messiah:
> grant us the faith to know you and love you,
> that we may be found beside you
> on the way of the cross,
> which is the path of glory.

COLLECT

Friday 15 April
Good Friday

Psalm 69
Genesis 22.1-18
John 19.38-end
or Hebrews 10.1-10

Genesis 22.1-18

'I will indeed bless you' (v.17)

All through the week's readings, we have been reminded of how deep the suspicion is that God is our enemy: how could we not suspect it, in a world as brutal as this? Today's story brings this right into the spotlight. The God Abraham has trusted suddenly demands a death, the death of what Abraham holds most precious, what speaks to him most directly of God's faithfulness.

So what does God want? Life or death?

All through the week's readings we have also been reminded of how we rediscover God's presence and freedom just when everything else falls away. Here too, it is as Abraham faces this most dreadful of deaths that suddenly what bursts upon him is the God who does not want death but life.

It's as though Abraham has to feel the unbearable *gravity* and preciousness of a human life, as he imagines the nightmare of being responsible for the death of the person he most loves, before he can see fully what human life means to *God* – how, in God's eyes, every human life is the life of a child loved without limit, for whom no risk, no cost, is too great.

So precious are human selves to God that God does not crush human freedom even at its most deluded and violent, and yet at one and the same time draws back the veil from his face to show the love that will not let go – of Abraham or Isaac or you and me. His will, his *passion*, is life for the world.

COLLECT

Almighty Father,
look with mercy on this your family
for which our Lord Jesus Christ was content to be betrayed
    and given up into the hands of sinners
    and to suffer death upon the cross;
who is alive and glorified with you and the Holy Spirit,
one God, now and for ever.

Psalm 142
Hosea 6.1-6
John 2.18-22

Saturday 16 April
Easter Eve

Hosea 6.1-6
'I desire steadfast love' (v.6)

We have been 'hewn', cut deeply, like stones from a quarry, by the words of the prophets. We have been invited to look at the violence and horror of the human world without any attempt to soften it – and to put into words the terrible suspicion that God is hostile or absent. We have been shown the full cost of human cruelty and rejection. We have been pushed to see more clearly the truth of human pain and human sin. It cuts deep.

At the heart of it all is, again and again, a revelation of something more than we can really imagine: the deeper truth that God cannot and will not be torn away from his creation. The future that God promises can't be imagined or controlled, but it is as sure as the expectation of the spring rains.

Within and beneath everything in creation is God's passion for life and joy. Nothing can separate us from this. And nothing can tear God away from the One who is the greatest of the prophets, the Son that God loves, the Word who is eternally with God. In the humanity which he lives out on earth, he absorbs the world's violence and hatred without ever passing it on. He does not crush or deny our dangerous freedom. And so he remains in his Father's heart, anchored in eternal love and life.

Death itself cannot defeat this. And if we come to stand where he stands, living in his Spirit, death cannot defeat us. We shall live before him.

COLLECT

Grant, Lord,
that we who are baptized into the death
of your Son our Saviour Jesus Christ
may continually put to death our evil desires
and be buried with him;
and that through the grave and gate of death
we may pass to our joyful resurrection;
through his merits,
who died and was buried and rose again for us,
your Son Jesus Christ our Lord.

Reflection by **Rowan Williams**   47

Morning Prayer – a simple form

Preparation

O Lord, open our lips
and our mouth shall proclaim your praise.

A prayer of thanksgiving for Lent *(for Passiontide see p. 50)*

Blessed are you, Lord God of our salvation,
to you be glory and praise for ever.
In the darkness of our sin you have shone in our hearts
to give the light of the knowledge of the glory of God
in the face of Jesus Christ.
Open our eyes to acknowledge your presence,
that freed from the misery of sin and shame
we may grow into your likeness from glory to glory.
Blessed be God, Father, Son and Holy Spirit.
Blessed be God for ever.

Word of God

Psalmody *(the psalm or psalms listed for the day)*

**Glory to the Father and to the Son
and to the Holy Spirit;
as it was in the beginning is now:
and shall be for ever. Amen.**

Reading from Holy Scripture *(one or both of the passages set for the day)*

Reflection

The Benedictus (The Song of Zechariah) *(see opposite page)*

Prayers

Intercessions – a time of prayer for the day and its tasks, the world and its need, the church and her life.

The Collect for the Day

The Lord's Prayer *(see p. 51)*

Conclusion

A blessing or the Grace *(see p. 51)*, or a concluding response

Let us bless the Lord
Thanks be to God

48

Benedictus (The Song of Zechariah)

1   Blessed be the Lord the God of Israel, ◆
     who has come to his people and set them free.

2   He has raised up for us a mighty Saviour, ◆
     born of the house of his servant David.

3   Through his holy prophets God promised of old ◆
     to save us from our enemies,
        from the hands of all that hate us,

4   To show mercy to our ancestors, ◆
     and to remember his holy covenant.

5   This was the oath God swore to our father Abraham: ◆
     to set us free from the hands of our enemies,

6   Free to worship him without fear, ◆
     holy and righteous in his sight
        all the days of our life.

7   And you, child, shall be called the prophet of the Most High, ◆
     for you will go before the Lord to prepare his way,

8   To give his people knowledge of salvation ◆
     by the forgiveness of all their sins.

9   In the tender compassion of our God ◆
     the dawn from on high shall break upon us,

10   To shine on those who dwell in darkness
        and the shadow of death, ◆
     and to guide our feet into the way of peace.

Luke 1.68-79

**Glory to the Father and to the Son
and to the Holy Spirit;
as it was in the beginning is now:
and shall be for ever. Amen.**

Seasonal Prayers of Thanksgiving

Passiontide

Blessed are you, Lord God of our salvation,
to you be praise and glory for ever.
As a man of sorrows and acquainted with grief
your only Son was lifted up
that he might draw the whole world to himself.
May we walk this day in the way of the cross
and always be ready to share its weight,
declaring your love for all the world.
Blessed be God, Father, Son and Holy Spirit.
Blessed be God for ever.

At Any Time

Blessed are you, creator of all,
to you be praise and glory for ever.
As your dawn renews the face of the earth
bringing light and life to all creation,
may we rejoice in this day you have made;
as we wake refreshed from the depths of sleep,
open our eyes to behold your presence
and strengthen our hands to do your will,
that the world may rejoice and give you praise.
Blessed be God, Father, Son and Holy Spirit.
Blessed be God for ever.

after Lancelot Andrewes (1626)

The Lord's Prayer and The Grace

Our Father in heaven,
hallowed be your name,
your kingdom come,
your will be done,
on earth as in heaven.
Give us today our daily bread.
Forgive us our sins
as we forgive those who sin against us.
Lead us not into temptation
but deliver us from evil.
For the kingdom, the power,
and the glory are yours
now and for ever.
Amen.

(or)

Our Father, who art in heaven,
hallowed be thy name;
thy kingdom come;
thy will be done;
on earth as it is in heaven.
Give us this day our daily bread.
And forgive us our trespasses,
as we forgive those who trespass against us.
And lead us not into temptation;
but deliver us from evil.
For thine is the kingdom,
the power and the glory,
for ever and ever.
Amen.

The grace of our Lord Jesus Christ,
and the love of God,
and the fellowship of the Holy Spirit,
be with us all evermore.
Amen.

An Order for Night Prayer (Compline)

The Lord almighty grant us a quiet night and a perfect end.
Amen.

Our help is in the name of the Lord
who made heaven and earth.

A period of silence for reflection on the past day may follow.

The following or other suitable words of penitence may be used

**Most merciful God,
we confess to you,
before the whole company of heaven and one another,
that we have sinned in thought, word and deed
and in what we have failed to do.
Forgive us our sins,
heal us by your Spirit
and raise us to new life in Christ. Amen.**

O God, make speed to save us.
O Lord, make haste to help us.

**Glory to the Father and to the Son
and to the Holy Spirit;
as it was in the beginning is now
and shall be for ever. Amen.
Alleluia.**

The following or another suitable hymn may be sung

Before the ending of the day,
Creator of the world, we pray
That you, with steadfast love, would keep
Your watch around us while we sleep.

From evil dreams defend our sight,
From fears and terrors of the night;
Tread underfoot our deadly foe
That we no sinful thought may know.

O Father, that we ask be done
Through Jesus Christ, your only Son;
And Holy Spirit, by whose breath
Our souls are raised to life from death.

The Word of God

One or more of Psalms 4, 91 or 134 may be used.

Psalm 134

1   Come, bless the Lord, all you servants of the Lord, ♦
     you that by night stand in the house of the Lord.

2   Lift up your hands towards the sanctuary ♦
     and bless the Lord.

3   The Lord who made heaven and earth ♦
     give you blessing out of Zion.

**Glory to the Father and to the Son
and to the Holy Spirit;
as it was in the beginning is now
and shall be for ever. Amen.**

Scripture Reading

*One of the following short lessons or another suitable
passage is read*

You, O Lord, are in the midst of us and we are called by your
name; leave us not, O Lord our God.

Jeremiah 14.9

(or)

Be sober, be vigilant, because your adversary the devil is
prowling round like a roaring lion, seeking for someone
to devour. Resist him, strong in the faith.

1 Peter 5.8,9

(or)

The servants of the Lamb shall see the face of God, whose name
will be on their foreheads. There will be no more night: they will
not need the light of a lamp or the light of the sun, for God will
be their light, and they will reign for ever and ever.

Revelation 22.4,5

Into your hands, O Lord, I commend my spirit.
Into your hands, O Lord, I commend my spirit.
For you have redeemed me, Lord God of truth.
I commend my spirit.
Glory to the Father and to the Son
and to the Holy Spirit.
Into your hands, O Lord, I commend my spirit.

Or, in Easter

Into your hands, O Lord, I commend my spirit.
  Alleluia, alleluia.
Into your hands, O Lord, I commend my spirit.
  Alleluia, alleluia.
For you have redeemed me, Lord God of truth.
Alleluia, alleluia.
Glory to the Father and to the Son
and to the Holy Spirit.
Into your hands, O Lord, I commend my spirit.
  Alleluia, alleluia.

Keep me as the apple of your eye.
Hide me under the shadow of your wings.

Gospel Canticle

Nunc Dimittis (The Song of Simeon)

Save us, O Lord, while waking,
and guard us while sleeping,
that awake we may watch with Christ
and asleep may rest in peace.

1   Now, Lord, you let your servant go in peace:
    your word has been fulfilled.

2   My own eyes have seen the salvation
    which you have prepared in the sight of every people;

3   A light to reveal you to the nations
    and the glory of your people Israel.

Luke 2.29-32

Glory to the Father and to the Son
and to the Holy Spirit;
as it was in the beginning is now
and shall be for ever. Amen.

Save us, O Lord, while waking,
and guard us while sleeping,
that awake we may watch with Christ
and asleep may rest in peace.

Prayers

Intercessions and thanksgivings may be offered here.

The Collect

Visit this place, O Lord, we pray,
and drive far from it the snares of the enemy;
may your holy angels dwell with us and guard us in peace,
and may your blessing be always upon us;
through Jesus Christ our Lord.
Amen.

The Lord's Prayer (see p. 51) may be said.

The Conclusion

In peace we will lie down and sleep;
for you alone, Lord, make us dwell in safety.

Abide with us, Lord Jesus,
for the night is at hand and the day is now past.

As the night watch looks for the morning,
so do we look for you, O Christ.

[Come with the dawning of the day
and make yourself known in the breaking of the bread.]

The Lord bless us and watch over us;
the Lord make his face shine upon us and be gracious to us;
the Lord look kindly on us and give us peace.
Amen.

REFLECTIONS FOR DAILY PRAYER
App

Make Bible study and reflection a part of your routine wherever you go with the Reflections for Daily Prayer App for Apple and Android devices.

Download the app for free from the App Store (Apple devices) or Google Play (Android devices) and receive a week's worth of reflections free. Then purchase a monthly, three-monthly or annual subscription to receive up-to-date content.

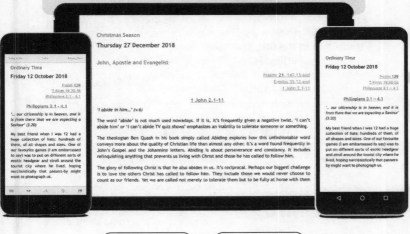

REFLECTIONS FOR SUNDAYS (YEAR C)

Reflections for Sundays offers over 250 reflections on the Principal Readings for every Sunday and major Holy Day in Year C, from the same experienced team of writers that have made *Reflections for Daily Prayer* so successful. For each Sunday and major Holy Day, they provide:

- full lectionary details for the Principal Service
- a reflection on each Old Testament reading (both Continuous and Related)
- a reflection on the Epistle
- a reflection on the Gospel.

This book also contains a substantial introduction to the Gospel of Luke, written by Paula Gooder.

£14.99 • 288 pages
ISBN 978 1 78140 039 5

Also available in Kindle and epub formats

REFLECTIONS ON THE PSALMS

£14.99 • 192 pages
ISBN 978 0 7151 4490 9

Reflections on the Psalms provides original and insightful meditations on each of the Bible's 150 Psalms.

Each reflection is accompanied by its corresponding Psalm refrain and prayer from the *Common Worship Psalter*, making this a valuable resource for personal or devotional use.

Specially written introductions by Paula Gooder and Steven Croft explore the Psalms and the Bible and the Psalms in the life of the Church.